30 DAYS:
A DEVOTIONAL FOR NEW RELATIONSHIPS

By:

MARCIE LYNN

Tate Publishing, LLC

Published in the United States of America
By TATE PUBLISHING, LLC

Book Design by TATE PUBLISHING, LLC.

Printed in the United States of America by
TATE PUBLISHING, LLC
127 East Trade Center Terrace
Mustang, OK 73064
(888) 361-9473

Publisher's Cataloging in Publication

Lynn, Marcie

30 Days / Marcie Lynn

Originally published in Mustang, OK:

TATE PUBLISHING:2004

1. Devotional 2. Dating

ISBN 1-9331484-2-X $9.95

First Printing: October   2004

DEDICATION

This devotional is dedicated to all Christian couples in new relationships. My prayer is that this will help you start off your relationship centered on Christ, and help you get to know yourself and your partner better.

ACKNOWLEDGEMENTS

I'd like to thank God, first and foremost, for being my rock and my soft place to fall. He is always there for me through all the sorrow and joy in my life. Without Him I would be nothing. I pray that He will use this devotional to His glory.

I'd like to thank my mom and dad for giving me a good Christian foundation to build my life on, and for being there through the good times and the bad.

I'd like to thank my pastor, Pastor Wilmer J. Olszewski, of the Hookstown Free Methodist Church for the support, input, and suggestions he has made to this devotional.

I'd like to thank Cheryl, Ginger, Helen, Lorie, Ruth, and others in my church who encouraged me to publish this devotional and follow God's leading.

I'd like to thank all my friends from the Christian Mingle website, who inspired and encouraged me to publish this devotional and I'd like to acknowledge a few specifically for taking the time to read through, comment, and give this book a test run for me: Confidante, Dony, Eagleswings, Pilate1, Ridgewood, and Thewaygirl.

TABLE OF CONTENTS

FOREWORD

As a Pastor, I recommend this devotional book to any couple who has just entered a new relationship. Although targeted primarily to young adults, this devotional could be used by teenagers or even older adults. One of the great benefits of this book is that it provides a practical way to follow the great commandments of Jesus. "Jesus replied, 'Love the Lord your God with all your heart and with all your soul and with all your mind. This is the first and greatest commandment. And the second is like it, Love your neighbor as yourself.'" (Matthew 22:37–39)

This is a devotional book which allows you and your partner to discover a personal relationship with God through scripture reading and prayer. Also, this is a book about new relationships and about how, while growing closer to the Lord, you can learn exciting new things about the other person. As you read, reflect and pray together. Using *30 Days* will give you the opportunity to be honest with one another and honesty is so important, especially in a new relationship.

The beautiful part of this devotional is that it includes scriptures, questions, and a devotional thought to consider. Marcie Lynn has taken the time to integrate the Bible with life experiences. There are many interesting things to learn about your new dating partner. You can discover likes and dislikes, favorite foods, and what stresses the other person is experiencing. Marcie has tested this devotional with friends who are in new relationships and they have enjoyed praying, reading, and learning about each other.

During my Pastoral ministry, I have conducted a couple hundred wedding services. Unfortunately, during that time I have met with far too many couples who barely knew each other let alone knew God. One of the things that I desire is that couples are prepared for their wedding day by knowing each other and by knowing God. This devotional by Marcie Lynn can become the stepping stone towards building a God-centered relationship. Whatever path your new relationship takes, one thing is sure, your relationship with the Lord will grow and you will always win by being closer to Him.

Wilmer J. Olszewski
Senior Pastor
Hookstown Free Methodist Church

DAY 1

- **How did you get your name?**

- **Do you like your name?**

- **Do you know the meaning of your name?**

Genesis 5:2 (NASB) He created them male and female, and He blessed them and named them Man in the day when they were created.

In the King James Version of the Bible, the word Man is translated as "Adam." In Hebrew, Adam, is derived from a word meaning "to be red." Adam, the first man, was formed from the red earth. However, Adam is also used as the generic name of the human race.

You are a part of Adam's family (that is, the human race) simply by being physically born. However, to become a part of God's family, you must be born again, by having faith in Jesus. This makes us all brothers and sisters in Christ.

Through being a part of God's family, you receive many privileges here on earth; however, you will receive much better rewards in eternity.

As part of God's family you should always be open with your brothers and sisters. You should discuss and share what God is doing for you, showing you, and teaching you. You should pray for each other and always encourage each other. You need to be there for each other and to really care for each other.

As you go through life, you need to remember that you are representing our Heavenly Father. You carry the family name. You need to be careful in how you act and what you say and you must always strive to bring honor to your family name.

DAY 2

* **Are you happy with who you are — not in your job, or life, but with who you are at the core? Why or why not?**

* **How do you feel about where you are in life?**

Romans 12:3 (MSG) . . . The only accurate way to understand ourselves is by what God is and by what he does for us, not by what we are and what we do for him.

Have you ever thought about how you really got to where you are? Have you thought about how you became the person you are? You are who you are because of a plan that God has for you. God makes each person unique, designed with His plan in mind. You were given your looks, your personality, your talents, and your location by God. You were born to just the right people, and raised by just the right people to make you who God wanted you to be. Think about that, your parents were hand picked by God. The people who raised you were hand picked by God. YOU were hand picked by God!

All the sorrow, trauma, and hard times you have gone through, although not easy, have shaped you in many ways. Through it all, God has been right there with you and has felt the pain you have gone through. All the joy, excitement, and good times you have experienced have also been used to shape who you are.

The next time you don't like something about yourself, go to God in prayer to see if it is something that you should accept or change. A lot of times, you will find that it is something that God has intentionally put into you and is something that He wants you to use as a witness to bring others into His family.

DAY 3

Name some of your favorites:

* **What is your favorite food—not type—what food item is your favorite?**

* **What is your favorite dessert?**

* **What is your favorite drink?**

* **What are some foods you DON'T like?**

* **What is your favorite color?**

Job 33:19–23 (MSG) Or, God might get their attention through pain, by throwing them on a bed of suffering, So they can't stand the sight of food, have no appetite for their favorite treats. They lose weight, wasting away to nothing, reduced to a bag of bones. They hang on the cliff-edge of death, knowing the next breath may be their last. But even then an angel could come, a champion—there are thousands of them!—to take up your cause . . .

Job thought that God was angry with him because of the afflictions brought to his body. Job couldn't even stand to see food, and couldn't bring himself to want his favorite treats.

Sometimes God afflicts your body for the good of your soul. An example of this would be Jesus. Jesus suffered great affliction to His body to save each and every one of us. He suffered immense pain to save our souls, YOUR soul. Nothing is of more value than your soul to God. God gave His only son to redeem your soul. Remember that at anytime, Jesus could have chosen to walk away and not pay that price, but He didn't. He CHOSE to suffer the pain inflicted on His body for all of mankind. Jesus is the Bread of Life.

The next time you are afflicted in body, try to see if there is something you can learn from the affliction for the good of your soul.

DAY 4

◆ What do you feel you truly deserve in this life?

Ezra 9:13 (NASB-U) After all that has come upon us for our evil deeds and our great guilt, since You our God have requited us less than our iniquities deserve, and have given us an escaped remnant as this . . .

Did Jesus deserve the suffering He endured? Did Jesus deserve to die on that cross? Did you deserve the sacrifice that Jesus made for you? Do you deserve to be forgiven of your sins? Do you deserve the patience that the Lord continually shows you?

The answer to all of these questions is a resounding NO. Have you ever wondered, "Is there an end to God's patience?" Well God has provided a never ending way for you to be forgiven and that is through the blood of His son, Jesus Christ. God's mercy and grace are unending.

However, you should not abuse the grace of God. You should give God all of your heart, mind, and soul. You need to be completely devoted to God. You need to strive everyday to live a life that is pleasing to God.

You need to love God and what God loves. You need to love others as you love yourself. You need to remember that you don't deserve anything that God gives you—He gives it to you because He loves you.

DAY 5

+ **What are some of your pet peeves?**

+ **What is something that you find offensive?**

+ **What is your reaction to the offense?**

Daniel 3:29 (NASB-U) Therefore I make a decree that any people, nation or tongue that speaks anything offensive against the God of Shadrach, Meshach and Abed-nego shall be torn limb from limb and their houses reduced to a rubbish heap, inasmuch as there is no other god who is able to deliver in this way.

In the past week, have you done anything that was offensive to God? Do you try to live a life that is pleasing to God?

What are some things that God finds offensive? Complaining (Numbers 11:1), pride, lying, and wicked imaginations (Proverbs 6:16–18). Would you like to change your answer to the first question?

As you go through your daily life, you need to remember that you are to love one another. God doesn't like it when you complain about others, when you are boastful about yourself, or when you lie to others. You need to remember what love is as defined in the Bible (1 Corinthians 13:4–8). Love is patient, kind, trustful, protects, hopes, and never ends. Love does not envy, does not boast, is not proud, is not rude, is not self-seeking, is not easily angered, and keeps no record of wrongdoing.

If you can remember these things and really try to put them into practice, then you will be living a life that is pleasing to God.

DAY 6

- **How long ago and under what circumstances did you find the Lord?**

- **What can you share today about your relationship with the Lord?**

1 John 4:14–15 (NASB) We have seen and testify that the Father has sent the Son to be the Savior of the world. Whoever confesses that Jesus is the Son of God, God abides in him, and he in God.

God has provided a way to himself through His son, Jesus Christ. You must believe in Jesus, acknowledge your belief with your mouth, and change the way you live your life. You show that you truly have the Lord in your heart by the way you live your life. If you profess to love God, and yet continue to be angry, have a quick temper, are revengeful, or are selfish, then you show your confession to be a lie.

People will say, "But Jesus got angry." Yes, Jesus did get angry, but when He got angry, it was never over something that happened to Him. Jesus only became angry over things that happened to other people, it wasn't a selfish anger.

We can learn a lot by looking at what Jesus DIDN'T get angry, revengeful, or selfish over. He didn't get angry because people didn't believe him. He didn't get angry when people thought He was a liar, a fraud, and a fake. He didn't get revengeful when people were out to kill him. He didn't even get angry when He was being beaten for your sin. And nowhere can you find less selfishness than when He was on the cross. While on the cross He asked for forgiveness for those who put him there and instead of calling ten thousand angels to free him, He stayed right there for you.

Is God abiding in you? Are you abiding in God? If so, then show it by the way you live and strive to be more like Jesus everyday.

DAY 7

- **How often do you laugh each day?**

- **What is your favorite joke or funny family story?**

Ecclesiastes 3:4 (MSG) A right time to cry and another to laugh, A right time to lament and another to cheer . . .

You can't spend every minute of your life smiling and laughing and having a good time, but you do need to live your life so that others will want to have what you have. You are free, you have eternal life, and you have the love of God in your heart. You need to share the good news with everyone.

Who would want to have what you have if you are always complaining, always whining, always gloomy, and always negative? Think about it—how do you feel when you get up in the morning and see a dark, dreary day? That's how you make people feel when you portray any of the above-mentioned qualities.

On the other hand, when you wake up and see a bright, shining day, you can't wait to get at things; you are cheerful and happy.

You need to spread this kind of joy and happiness to others. Just by having a smile on your face and a good word to say you can be a witness of Christ's love to others. They will want to know what makes you so happy. They will want to have what you have.

So get out there and do God's work with a smile!

DAY 8

◆ When you have nothing to do, what do you do?

Exodus 5:17 (NASB) But he said, "You are lazy, very lazy; therefore you say, 'Let us go and sacrifice to the Lord.'"

You were not sent into the world to be lazy. God put you on this earth to serve others. By serving others, you are actually serving God. God gave the life of His only son to purchase your salvation—you owe God your life.

If you do not show your love to others through your actions and service and are only concerned with your own needs, then Christ is really not in your life. God designed you for service, and if your heart is His, you will want to serve.

God gives you abilities which you can use to help others. No ability is too small or too large to be used in the service of the Lord.

Some day you will stand before God. How much of your time will God see that you spent on yourself, and how much will He see that you spent on others? Do you want to have to say that you "didn't have time to serve," that you were "too busy?"

Spend any idle time you may have by serving others or learning more about God by reading His Word. Don't waste your idle time. You are only on this earth for a short time, but you will be spending eternity with God and your brothers and sisters in Christ.

DAY 9

- **What is one of the greatest times of trial that you have faced?**

- **How did you make it through that time?**

2 Samuel 22:3–4 (MSG) My God—the high crag where I run for dear life, hiding behind the boulders, safe in the granite hideout; My mountaintop refuge, He saves me from ruthless men. I sing to God the praise-lofty, and find myself safe and saved.

God is with you in everything. He is present even during your greatest trials and dangers. Even though you are attacked here on earth by your enemies, God is with you. One day you will be rid of all of these trials in eternity, but until then, you must persevere.

The greatest test of your faith comes during times of trouble. You need to praise the Lord at those times. God is your rock and you can trust in Him. God has good plans for you and works everything out (even your trials and troubles) for your good.

Sometimes you need to face your fears, to trust in the Lord and take a step of faith. God may be urging you to try something new, to expand your service, or to stretch your faith. You need to be aware of what God is leading you to do and trust in him completely.

God IS love and love never fails.

DAY 10

* **How do you define success?**

* **What would you say are your top five priorities at this point in your life?**

Matthew 7:7 (NASB) Ask, and it will be given to you; seek, and you will find; knock, and it will be opened to you.

Jesus says that all you have to do is ask and it will be given unto you. You need to seek God through prayer. God is all-knowing. He knows what is best for you, what you need, and what your desires are. If the things you ask Him for are good for you, God will grant them to you.

God also knows the best "when" for you. You may pray and pray and pray, and appear to receive no answer; however, God's timing is always perfect. God always listens, He always hears your prayers and He always answers. God just doesn't always answer with the answer you want or in your timing.

You need to remember that God knows all. You may think something is good for you, but God knows what is *truly* good for you.

God is not going to give you something that is going to be hurtful to you. When you take things out of God's hands and put them into your own is when you end up in a place that is not good for you. You should always seek God and what God wants—only then will you truly receive God's great rewards for your life.

DAY 11

♦ **Do you think you are showing respect in this relationship? In what ways?**

Ephesians 5:33 (NASB) Nevertheless, each individual among you also is to love his own wife even as himself, and the wife must see to it that she respects her husband.

Do you think this verse should only apply to those who are married? Wouldn't it be great if it applied to those who are starting a relationship, beginning to date, or even those who are just starting out as friends? You may think that love is a big word to be using so early in a relationship, but is it really?

In the Bible, you are instructed to love one another and to treat others as you would want to be treated. Why should you wait to start loving in this way? If you are a brother or sister in Christ, then you should already "love" others.

The word reverence means respect. Is this something that you need to wait to be married to show? No. You should show respect to each other as fellow Christians regardless of whether or not you are married to the person.

Love and respect don't just belong in marriage—they belong in the world as part of your everyday living. Love and respect should grow, not start, when you get married.

DAY 12

♦ **What do you think is the biggest setback or failure you've experienced?**

Luke 22:32 (NASB-U) . . . but I have prayed for you, that your faith may not fail; and you, when once you have turned again, strengthen your brothers.

Satan is always out to destroy or weaken your faith. As you get caught up in life's successes, you sometimes forget where you came from. When you do, you may gain a false sense of security or confidence. This is when Satan chooses to strike. This is when you are most likely to experience the farthest fall and the biggest failure. And at this time, when you are at your most vulnerable point, is when you become the most susceptible to doubting your faith and doubting God.

Very often, when you start doing something really good for the Kingdom of God, you will be assaulted and tested by Satan. This is when things will start to come apart, battles will be waged, and lots of work will be required to get the good accomplished. You need to be in prayer, asking for God's will to be done and asking that God close off those doors that He does not desire you to walk through. This way you can be assured to stay on God's path for you and not stray. If you don't stay in prayer and seek God's will, you may end up fighting battles that were only placed there as a distraction from the good you are trying to accomplish.

You need to be continually in prayer against the evils of the world that are all around you at all times. You cannot do battle without the power of God with you.

DAY 13

- **Is there a negative comment from your past that stays with you?**

- **How does it make you feel?**

Psalm 38:12–15 (MSG) My competitors blacken my name, devoutly they pray for my ruin. But I'm deaf and mute to it all, ears shut, mouth shut. I don't hear a word they say, don't speak a word in response. What I do, God, is wait for you, wait for you my Lord, my God—you will answer!

When someone says something negative about you, you need to turn immediately to God. You need to leave those negative remarks unnoticed, and seek the quiet reassurance of God. Those who are not believers are not going to change because they are not under the direction of God. They do not have God's love in their hearts.

If you seek God in these times, you will make your trouble useful to you. You can learn to wait on God and learn to seek His relief. You cannot control how others act or what others say. You can only control yourself and how you react to those things. You can continue to dwell on what was said or done and let that take hold of you, or you can let it go and let God's love get you through. Sometimes the only way to love someone is to allow God to put that love in your heart— you cannot always do it on your own.

DAY 14

♦ **What were some of the major factors that attracted you to me?**

Genesis 2:18 (NASB) Then the Lord God said, "It is not good for the man to be alone; I will make him a helper suitable for him."

God designed you to be in relationships, first with God, and then with each other. When you look for someone to spend time with, you look for certain qualities. You look for things you have in common and for things that you enjoy doing together. However, you need to look deeper than just what you see on the outside.

You should look for someone who is committed, equal, consistent, and faithful. You should find someone who wants to serve and love, and someone who brings out the best in you. You should seek someone who will put your needs before his/her own. You should look for someone with a good sense of humor because life can deal some really hard blows and you should also find someone who is able to communicate clearly, honestly, and sincerely with you.

You should look for someone who

knows what matters in life and is focused on that. You should seek someone who has a balanced sense of direction in life and someone who has good values and morals.

Most importantly, you should look for someone who is a true person of faith and who shows that faith in his/her life. That is, someone who shows spiritual fruit on a regular basis (Galatians 5:22–23), and someone who knows what love is and shows it (I Corinthians 13:4–8).

Before you look for all of these things in someone else, you should make sure that you have these things within yourself.

DAY 15

- **What do you think are five of your best qualities?**

- **What are five of your worst?**

- **Have you ever taken a spiritual gifts inventory? If so, what are your spiritual gifts?**

- **How are you using your gifts to serve the Lord?**

Matthew 25:21 (NASB) "His master said to him, 'Well done, good and faithful slave. You were faithful with a few things, I will put you in charge of many things; enter into the joy of your master.'"

God has given gifts to every one of His children, and that includes you! He wants you to use these gifts to help others in His Kingdom. If you are a good and faithful servant who uses your talents wisely, you will receive great rewards. Doing good does not get you into Heaven; it is something that you should do because you want to, not because you will receive anything in return for it.

Each and every one of God's children

has been given certain character qualities that can benefit the workings of the Lord's family. There are many areas within the church that require certain qualities. Some people are good at dealing with babies, while others are better at dealing with children or teens. Some people enjoy spending time with older adults. Some like to send out cards to those who need encouragement or to those who are sick. Still others like to make phone calls. Some enjoy being in front of the crowd and up on stage, while others prefer to remain in the background.

Look around your church and see if there are any areas of ministry in which you could put your qualities and characteristics to good use. God calls you to be a part of His body and to work for the advancement of His Kingdom. What part of the body could you be?

DAY 16

- ## What is it that really makes you feel valuable?

Matthew 10:31 (NASB) So do not fear; you are more valuable than many sparrows.

God knows you and cares for you. You are of great value to him and He watches over you. He cared for you even before you were born.

God decided what race you would be, what color of hair and eyes you would have, what you would look like, what talents and short-comings you would have, what type of personality and characteristics you would have, and everything else about you. God formed you just the way He wanted.

God knew where and when you would be born, who your parents would be, where you would live, and for how long you would live there. God has planned how long you will live on earth and even when and where you will die.

God does not make mistakes. He makes each of us perfect in His sight. He loves each and every one of us because we are His children.

DAY 17

- **What is your favorite holiday? Why?**

- **How do you spend your holidays? (Christmas Eve, Christmas Day, Thanksgiving, New Years, Easter?)**

- **How do you see the holidays working when you are in a relationship?**

Esther 9:19 (NASB-U) Therefore the Jews of the rural areas, who live in the rural towns, make the fourteenth day of the month Adar a holiday for rejoicing and feasting and sending portions of food to one another.

The Jews at this time were acting to strengthen one another, to stand together against their enemies. We, as brothers and sisters in Christ, should stand together in one spirit and in one mind against the enemy that attacks our soul because when we are under attack, we can become discouraged and then our faith is at risk.

Too often we are a house divided by petty differences. We allow the enemy to divide and wear us down. We allow gossip to sway how we think of certain people. We allow the way someone looks to determine how we treat them. We allow little inconveniences to keep us from enjoying or attending celebrations with our fellow Christians.

You need to remember to celebrate the great gifts, mercies, and grace that your Lord gives to you on every occasion. You need to remember that the one standing next to you is your brother or sister in faith and that you have a common goal of praising and thanking God.

DAY 18

- **When you are in a disagreement, how do you react?**

- **What is something that makes you angry?**

James 1:19–20 (NASB) This you know, my beloved brethren. But everyone must be quick to hear, slow to speak and slow to anger; for the anger of man does not achieve the righteousness of God.

The worst thing you can do when you get into a disagreement is to become angry. Once you are angry, you have a hard time listening to the other person. If you are angry, you will also have a hard time hearing God.

God calls you to love one another and to love your enemies. Love is not easily angered, instead it is long-suffering. You may find yourself at a point where you say to the Lord that you cannot love a certain person. When you reach this point, you have to allow God to love him/her through you. You must allow God to fill you up with His life-giving love, so that you can then carry His love to others and pour it out onto their lives no matter how difficult it may be.

Most importantly, you need to forget your sinful instincts! By nature, your instinct wants to set you on a course for destruction. Your feelings can lie to you. You shouldn't allow them to set the tone or the pace for your relationships. Instead, you need to allow God's Word, His patience, and His selflessness to guide you.

DAY 19

- ◆ **Do you think that you show the fruits of the Spirit in your everyday living?**

- ◆ **Which do you think would be your strongest fruit and which would be your weakest?**

Galatians 5:22–23 (NIV) But the fruit of the Spirit is love, joy, peace, patience, kindness, goodness, faithfulness, gentleness, self-control; against such things there is no law.

When you accept Jesus as your Lord and Savior, you should start to grow in the Holy Spirit. When you look at a Christian's life, you should be able to see the fruits of the Spirit at work.

To be a Christian does not mean that you simply cease from doing evil and sinful things—you must also learn to do good things. You have a new life in Christ; you must strive to be more like Jesus everyday. By allowing the Holy Spirit to have control of your mind, body, and soul, you will show others that you truly are a Christian.

Everyday you should take an inventory of what your life is showing others. You need to think about what fruit you need to work on. Because you are human, you will never be able to be exactly like Christ; however, with the help of the Holy Spirit, you can work toward being the best Christian that you can possibly be. You are a witness to unbelievers. Remember that you represent God to others and you want them to want what you have.

DAY 20

- **Have you ever felt separated from the love of God?**

- **In what ways have you experienced the love of God?**

- **Have you been in other relationships in which you were separated from love?**

Romans 8:38–39 (NIV) For I am convinced that neither death nor life, neither angels nor demons, neither the present nor the future, nor any powers, neither height nor depth, nor anything else in all creation, will be able to separate us from the love of God that is in Christ Jesus our Lord.

Jesus paid it all; He paid the entire cost for your sins, and nothing can ever take that away. The debt is paid in full. God's love for you was manifested through His giving His own son to suffer and die for you and nothing could ever do away with that kind of love.

Jesus made a conscious choice to suffer and die for you. He did not have to do anything for you. Jesus healed the sick, brought the dead back to life, and performed many miracles. Do you not believe that He could have walked away from the beatings, the suffering, the pain, the agony, and the cross?

You may lose loved ones, family, friends, possessions, homes, money, etc. Any earthly thing you can think of can be lost. You can even lose your earthly life! But you can never lose the love of God. When all those things are gone, God's love will still remain.

DAY 21

- **Do you think you spend enough time with Jesus in prayer?**

- **When do you pray?**

- **How comfortable are you at leading prayer in a group?**

- **How can I pray for you tonight?**

Psalm 55:17 (NIV) Evening, morning and noon I cry out in distress, and He hears my voice.

Prayer is a conversation with God. God wants to hear from you often—you can never come to Him too much. You should pray continually, giving thanks for big things as well as for small things. You should ask for help with big problems as well as with small problems. You should ask for guidance in big decisions as well as in small decisions. God is always listening and He will always answer you.

In the Bible you are told to offer up prayer for: kings, people in authority, ministers, the church, men, masters, servants, children, friends, fellow-countrymen, the sick, the persecuted, your enemies, those who envy you, those who forsake you, and those who murmur against God.

You should pray for others. You are a part of the family of God and you are to love and care for each other. Part of that loving and caring involves coming to God with intercessory prayer.

In the same way that you should pray for others, you should also seek out others to pray for you. You should bring your requests to others so that they may pray in agreement with you. There can never be too many people praying for you. Christ promises that where two or three are gathered together in His name, He will be among them (Matthew 18:20).

There are no rules set down in the Bible regarding the manner or attitude in which you must pray. Many positions are mentioned: kneeling, falling prostrate, spreading out of hands, and standing. The important thing is that you pray. It doesn't matter what position you are in, when you do it, or where you are. You just need to pray.

DAY 22

* **Do you sometimes feel that the Lord is not listening to you when you pray?**

* **Do you find it easy or difficult to trust God?**

Job 22:27 (NASB) You will pray to Him, and He will hear you; And you will pay your vows.

God always hears your prayers. He doesn't always answer them in the way or the timing that you would like, but He always hears them. Sometimes God answers with what you request, sometimes He answers with something other than what you have requested, sometimes He answers beyond your expectations, and sometimes His answer is just plain, "No." Sometimes He answers immediately, sometimes He answers in a few days, and sometimes the wait can be a long time.

In Proverbs 3:5 (NASB) you are told to: "Trust in the Lord with all your heart, And do not lean on your own understanding." This can be the hardest thing to do, but you must trust God. He has promised to always be there for you. He only wants the best for you and He knows what "the best" is so much better than you do.

DAY 23

- **How do you usually react when you are disappointed or discouraged?**

- **What can I do to help you when you're feeling down?**

Job 10:1 (MSG) "I can't stand my life—I hate it! I'm putting it all out on the table, all the bitterness of my life—I'm holding back nothing."

In this verse you see that Job had become weary and discouraged and was starting to complain. Despite this, he never blamed God for his troubles. He certainly wanted to be relieved of his afflictions though and so he laid them all out on the table before God. He told God everything that he was thinking and feeling. You too can be just as honest with God; you don't have to like everything that happens to you in your life and you don't have to be afraid to tell God how you really feel.

God allows afflictions in your life for a reason. You need to pray for understanding of what that reason is so that you can repent and ask for forgiveness. However, you should not harbor hard thoughts or feelings towards God.

God will use the hard times in your life to shape and sharpen you, if you allow Him to do so. You should continue to praise God even during the toughest and hardest of times. You must always praise God for He is good, all the time.

DAY 24

- **Who in your family are you the closest to? Why?**

- **If you don't have any close family, who are the closest people to you? Why?**

- **Is there someone in your life who is or was a spiritual parent / mentor? What qualities do / did that person possess that you are now trying to possess?**

2 Timothy 1:5 (NASB) For I am mindful of the sincere faith within you, which first dwelt in your grandmother Lois and your mother Eunice, and I am sure that it is in you as well.

Faith is a living principle to those who are true believers. It is faith that will help a true believer to stand against any storm that blows into his/her life. Lois and Eunice were successful at instilling this type of faith into Timothy during his upbringing. Throughout the Bible and in life, you can find examples of many people who have had early, valuable teachings on faith by their mother, grandmother, or another female relative. In addition to godly teaching, prayer is another powerful influence on young believers. Praying for the next generation is essential as the world turns darker and colder around you.

As you get older, you should become more and more aware of how your life may be influencing those around you, especially younger people. Just because you are not someone's mother or father, doesn't mean that you do not have influence on a young adult, a teen, or a child.

If you are a parent, you have all the more responsibility for what you are teaching as you bring up the next generation of God's children. You must strive everyday to give your children a positive role model to emulate. Every action you take will shout something to someone; therefore, you really need to think about what you are saying with your life.

DAY 25

♦ **Would you be shocked if I brought you flowers or some other gift for no reason at all?**

♦ **Do you prefer to be surprised in front of friends or privately?**

Matthew 7:11 (NIV) If you, then, though you are evil, know how to give good gifts to your children, how much more will your Father in heaven give good gifts to those who ask him!

By praying, you can obtain what you need. However, you need to be very serious and earnest in your prayers and you need to pray often. You need to seek God for guidance.

Whatever you pray for has been promised to be given to you, if God sees that it will be good for you. Would you expect God, our Father, to give you something that would be hurtful or harmful to you? No, of course not.

If earthly parents are ready to give to their children what they ask for, why would you be surprised that your Heavenly Father would do the same? Parents give to their children what is good for them, and withhold what is bad for them. As earthly parents, people can tend to be too giving to their children and thus spoil them; God however, is much wiser. God knows your every need, your every desire, and exactly what you need.

God always hears your prayers and always gives you an answer. And when God answers, it is always with your best interest at heart and it is always within the great plan that He has for you. Sometimes you are even surprised by what God gives you, for His blessings can go far beyond any expectations that you may have had.

DAY 26

♦ **How do you "hear" from God?**

John 16:12–14 (NASB-U) I have many more things to say to you, but you cannot bear them now. But when He, the Spirit of truth, comes, He will guide you into all the truth; for He will not speak on His own initiative, but whatever He hears, He will speak; and He will disclose to you what is to come. He will glorify Me, for He will take of Mine and will disclose it to you.

God speaks to you through the Holy Spirit, but there are many other forms in which He speaks to you as well.

One way God can speak to you is through the reading of His word, the Bible. The Word of God has been given to us by divine inspiration of the Holy Spirit speaking through His prophets and disciples and many times as you read it you will be able to sense God speaking to you through the scriptures. God can also speak to you through wisdom. He has given you the ability to learn from your past experiences which can help you gain knowledge that you can apply to future instances. He can also speak to you through dreams, visions, and prophecy; however these are less common ways.

Another way God can speak to you is by confirming something that you've heard through another person. Often times God will give someone a word of advice to give you that matches what you already feel in your own spirit.

Yet another way that God can speak to you is through your inner conscience, that is, you just know when you are not doing the right thing. You can be convicted of your sin in your conscience. You can look at something and just "know" that it is wrong.

Finally, God can speak to you through the peace that passes all understanding. When you have a peace about something, you know that you are on the right path. Satan cannot give you that peace, his peace will only last a short time. If in doubt, you need to pray and wait upon the Lord. Satan's peace will leave you, but God's peace will remain. If you are not at peace about something, you need to seek God's guidance through prayer until you find that peace.

DAY 27

* **What is something that makes you frustrated?**

* **Do you have friends whom you seek advice from in those times of frustration?**

* **Do you have friends who seek your advice?**

Proverbs 15:22 (NASB-U) Without consultation, plans are frustrated, But with many counselors they succeed.

You need to take time to plan out and discuss things before taking action. The old saying, "Two heads are better than one," is quite true. You should always seek wise counsel on any plans that you intend to make. You need to surround yourself with brothers and sisters in Christ who will discuss, guide, and pray for you on a daily basis.

Life can be hard, especially when you are facing things on your own. This can create frustration in your life. Praying for and seeking the will of God can relieve these frustrations, giving you a peace that passes all understanding. This peace assures you that the message is truly from God. If you are feeling frustrations, you need to turn to God—don't proceed if peace isn't there. You do not need to explain to anyone why you don't have peace, sometimes you will not know.

You need to obey your sense of right and wrong and resist things that your inner self is uncomfortable with. Satan cannot give you peace, but God can give and take peace from you, letting you know whether or not you are on track with His will.

You need to take your time, pray about things, and allow excitement to disappear. This excitement can cause you to have a false peace. Over time, however, that peace created by excitement alone will go away, allowing you to feel God's direction in your life.

DAY 28

- **Up to this point, what image, object, or metaphor has best described your life?**

Luke 6:39–40 (MSG) He quoted a proverb: "Can a blind man guide a blind man? Wouldn't they both end up in the ditch? An apprentice doesn't lecture the master. The point is to be careful who you follow as your teacher."

Jesus often used parables to teach with because they were easy to understand and were easy for His followers to apply to their lives.

In this particular parable found in Luke chapter 6, Christ is warning that you should be careful who you follow for if you follow evil, then you will surely be brought to destruction.

You need to be a person of light so that people of light will be drawn to you and so that people of darkness will not be able to tolerate the truth that you embody (John 3:19–21). This will allow you to be surrounded by good Christian people.

DAY 29

- **What are some changes you have experienced since you became a believer?**

- **Have others noticed a change in you? What is that change?**

Acts 3:19 (MSG) Now it's time to change your ways! Turn to face God so He can wipe away your sins, pour out showers of blessing to refresh you, and send you the Messiah He prepared for you, namely, Jesus.

When you accept Jesus as your Savior, you should experience a change. You should be refreshed by the sense of Christ's pardoning love. You should feel charged and on fire for the Lord. A heavy burden should be lifted from your shoulders as you are forgiven for all of your sins.

You should begin to live your life for God, seeking His will and His guidance. You should become servants to those around you, seeking places to teach and to work for others. You should want to spread the Gospel.

Others should begin to see the light of

Jesus shining in you. Your attitude should change and you should start becoming more like Jesus—more forgiving, more patient, and more kind.

God is love and you should begin to show that love to all because you are now a part of the family of God.

DAY 30

- **What is the driving force of your life?**

- **What do think it should be?**

- **What do you think your purpose in life is? Why?**

2 Corinthians 5:17 (NASB) Therefore if anyone is in Christ, he is a new creature; the old things passed away; behold, new things have come.

There are a lot of things that can drive your life. You can be driven by resentment, anger, fear, guilt, material things, need for acceptance, approval by others, peer pressure, and so on.

When you accept Jesus, you are given a new life. You should chase away these driving forces and focus on a life driven by God. Admittedly, this is a really hard thing to do because everyday life has a tendency to try and catch you in its current and sweep you down river.

When you take the time to find out what God's purpose is for your life though, your life can become much easier to live. Once you find your purpose, the current takes you right where you need to be and you don't have to fight it any longer.

God created you with special talents, abilities, and gifts to use to His glory. You can bring glory to God by enjoying Him, by worshiping Him, by praising Him, by giving yourself to Him, by loving Him and the things He loves (especially other believers), by striving everyday to become a little more like Him, by showing the fruits of the spirit, by loving as He has told you to, by using your gifts and abilities to serve others, and by spreading the good news of God's grace and mercy.

Contact Marcie Lynn
or order more copies of this book at

TATE PUBLISHING, LLC

127 East Trade Center Terrace
Mustang, Oklahoma 73064

(888) 361 - 9473

Tate Publishing, LLC

www.tatepublishing.com